ENTREPRENEUR-IZM

EMPLOYEE TO ENTREPRENEUR

"WORKING YOUR WAY OFF THE JOB"

by Tre' Gatewood

ISBN: 979-8-218551896 (Paperback)
Library of congress cataloging-in-publication data is Available:
Library of Congress Control Number: 2024923985

Property of Entrepreneurizm & Dogg Deep Enterprize
Published by Dogg Deep Publishing House
Book Cover by Enterprize Printing & Design
Illustrations by Enterprize Printing & Design
Printed by Enterprize Printing & Design in Memphis, TN
Memphis, TN 38141
www.DoggDeep.com

Entrepreneur IZM

ISM = Way of turning a *verb* into a *noun*

Terror Terror**ism**
Criticize Critic**ism**
Tour Tour**ism**
Exorcist Exorc**ism**

The Action / Process / Result of doing something
ENTREPRENEUR**ISM**
Religion / Idealism / Systems of thought

Rac**ism**
Sex**ism**
Capital**ism**
Hindu**ism**

Entrepreneur IZM

Table of Contents

Dedication

INTRODUCTION pg.15

CHAPTER 1: MINDSET
First Thing First pg.21
Discovering Your Dream pg.27
Unlearn and Relearn pg.32
Train Your Brain pg.36

CHAPTER 2: THE PLAN
Proper Planning pg.45
Finding Your Lane pg.50
Listen to You pg.55

CHAPTER 3: FOUNDATION
Build Strong pg.61
Your Identity pg.64
The Power of Networking pg.68
Resources over Money pg.70

CHAPTER 4: THE CHOICE
Chances and Choices pg.77
Fear pg.79
Sacrifice pg.82
Patients pg.83

CHAPTER 5: THE DOING
The 4 Check System pg.89
Tips x Advice x Game pg.91
Money Management... pg.96

INCLUDES (Resources)

The Dream Discovering Exercise pg.28

The Habit Replacement Worksheet pg.39

The Skill vs Talent Analysis pg.49

The Business Mathematical Formula pg.51

The Foundation Building Checklist pg.73

OUTRO

V

vi

Dedication

I chose to put the dedications first because most of my family and friends have literally never read a whole book in their entire lives. So if I put it at the end, their asses might never get to see thier names, LOL! So, here we go...

To my Family: My mother and sister who raised me and showed me the value of hard work. My mother is an avid reader and once told me something that is one of the truest things I have ever heard in my life. She said, "You can travel anywhere in the world by reading a book." She moved up from the projects of Westside Chicago with no college education, to a middle-class neighborhood and a good paying job in corporate America, that quote stuck with me and proved to be true. I remember my sister working three jobs at the same time (Sonic, Mrs. Winners, and FedEx) right after graduating high school and already having a child. THE HARDEST WORKING PEOPLE I KNOW ON EARTH!

To the Gatewood, Irby & Smith Family: My grandma Ella Mae, the foundation and backbone of the family, my Aunties Helen, Linda and Brenda, and my Uncles Marvin, Kirt, and Leon who gave me the smoothness and hardness I needed to maneuver with my head held high in confidence. To my little sister Khadiah and all my cousins on both sides. Y'all always kept me motivated and grounded. My Godmother Melissa and My Godfather, Barber, pastor, & friend, Terry Gathright. I met Mr. Gathright when I was 17 years old when I was completely lost in life. I didn't know if I wanted to be an entrepreneur, an employee, a pimp, a drug dealer, or a junkie. But It was him who saw something in me and made me understand that NO MATTER what you are or want to be, you must be a MAN before anything. Ever since then, that's the only path I have wanted to travel. Thank you for saving my life, Mr. Terry!

My mentors Sol Holland and the one and only Ms. Rose Fries. I could write an entire book on the impact Ms. Fries has made on my life as a friend, teacher, counselor, connector, and Rock! I know no obstacle is impossible with her in my corner and that confidence literally gives me superpowers. Ms.Fries, thank you for changing my life! To my best friends Jesse, Aubrey, Jack, Kay, Bobby, Jacob, JJ, Troy, Derrick, Zo, Ja & Mike, Sol, Marietta, Bridget, Foy, Daniel, Tim, Elgen and to my nephews Robert, Alenceo, Rodney, Semaj, Baby Charles, and Ben, to nieces Lisa, Shyionna, Shayla, Aniya, Baby Angel and to my god-daughter Elizabeth-Eugene. We did it!! Every step of the way y'all have been with me. From my lowest point to my highest, you've seen the real me, so you know the power of "change without changing"! I changed my life for sure, but "I'll" never change. Y'all taught me everything I know, so now it's y'all's turn to turn up. We are forever Dogg Deep!

To anyone who went to school with me, worked, or

hustled with me. To my TCAT, Crew One & ARO Family. To my city Memphis, to my neighborhood Hickory Hill. I carry you everywhere I go. And lastly, to my guardian angels, Grandfather Eugene Gatewood, Granddad Jack, Auntie Pam & Sherri, Granny Ina Jo Graham, & Grandma Gladys. My sister Sherrina and to my right-hand man James Mitchell. Not a day goes by that I don't think about and miss you all. The lessons taught will always be applied and never forgotten. I won't let you down!

This book is for anyone with a dream but don't know how they're going to achieve it. For every "**F**" student with "**A+**" ambitions. ***For the Lost ones...***

Now Let's Go!

SOCIAL AND ACADEMIC BEHAVIOR

CONDUCT AND WORK HABITS
E - Excellent   N - Needs Improvement
S - Satisfactory   U - Unsatisfactory

INDICATORS (Sub-Headings)
✓ Denotes Improvement Needed

	REPORTING PERIODS						FINAL
	1	2	3	4	5	6	
CONDUCT	N	N	N	E	S	E	S
Respects rights and property of self and others		✓		✓			
Obeys rules		✓	✓				
Assumes responsibility		✓		✓			
Respects authority							
Practices self-control							
WORK HABITS	N	N	N	N	N	N	
Tasks at appropriate times							
Asks appropriate questions							
Works and plays well with others							
Shows effort		✓		✓			
Pays attention		✓					
Listens and follows directions							
Stays on task		✓		✓			
Works independently		✓		✓			
Uses time and materials wisely		✓		✓			
Brings necessary materials							
Completes classwork in an accurate and timely manner		✓		✓		✓	
Submits homework on time		✓		✓		✓	

ATTENDANCE

							TOTAL
Days present	30	30	29	30	29	27	175
Days absent	0	1	0	0	1	3	4
Times tardy	0	1	0	0	1	2	4

Pupils who are absent or tardy must present a written excuse signed by parent or guardian. Irregular attendance affects progress.

REPORT OF : **EUGENE L. GATEWOOD**
PIN :

Grade/Section

Elementary School Report Card

Report of

TEACHER COMMENTS

1. Trey could do better if he applied him-self academically and use his time well.

☐ Teacher Requests Conference

2. Trey needs to work on staying focused and respect his classmates. He is improving in some areas.

☐ Teacher Requests Conference

3. Continue to work with Trey on taking pride in his work and not playing at school.

☐ Teacher Requests Conference

4. Perfect Attendance!

☐ Teacher Requests Conference

5. Trey is showing some improvement.

☐ Teacher Requests Conference

6. Have a great summer!

☐ Teacher Requests Conference

ACADEMIC SUBJECTS

SUBJECTS	REPORTING PERIODS						FINAL
	1	2	3	4	5	6	
Reading (1-6)	C	C	B	C	B	B	B
Composition (1-6)	C	C	B	C	B	B-	B
Grammar (1-6)			B		B	B	B
Spelling (1-6)	C	B-	B	B	B	B	B
Mathematics (1-6)	C	D	B	F	C	B	B-
*Science (3-6)	C	C	B		B	B	B
*Social Studies (3-6)	C	C	B	B	B	B	B

ACADEMIC GRADING SYSTEM

93-100	A	Excellent
85-92	B	Good
76-84	C	Average
70-75	D	Below Average
0-69	F	Failure

* Grading Legend for Grades 1 and 2: E, S, N, U

SPECIAL SUBJECTS

SUBJECTS (Grades 1-6)	REPORTING PERIODS						FINAL
	1	2	3	4	5	6	
Art	U	N	N	S	N	S	N
Computer Education	S	S	S	S	S	S	S
Handwriting	S	E	S	S	S	S	S
Health	S	E	E	E	E	S	S
Physical Education	S	S	N	E	S	S	S
Music							
Spanish			E				

SPECIAL SUBJECTS GRADING SYSTEM

The following marks indicate your child's interest, attitude, participation and proficiency in special areas.

E - Excellent   S - Satisfactory   N - Needs Improvement   U - Unsatisfactory

*A check (✓) in this column indicates that grades in this subject have been recorded in terms of the student's ability and effort in relationship to achievement as defined by the student's IEP

Gatewood, Eugene Lucious   Page: 1

Student ID: ~~████████~~   Six Weeks: 0.83333
Grade: 6 09   N Parrish   Birth Date: 5/15/89
                                                Retain: N

Course	Per	1st 6Wk	2nd 6Wk	3rd 6Wk	1sm Exm	1sm Avg	4th 6Wk	5th 6Wk	6th 6Wk	2sm Exm	2sm Avg	Yrs Avg
Language Arts 6	2	76	77	70	70	74						
Mathematics 6	3	23	50	62	68	48						
Social Studies 6	4	60	65	59	57	61						
Reading 6	5	76	73	74	73	74						
Band 6 - 180	6	77	88	91		85						
Science 6	7	80	78	66	60	74						

```
93-100 A-Excellent       I   Incomplete
85- 92 B-Good           EX   EXEMPT
76- 84 C-Average
70- 75 D-Poor
 0- 69 F-Failure
```

					Attendance			
					Current		YTD	
Course	Teacher	Attmpt Credit	Con dct		Abs	Tar	Abs	Tar
Language Arts 6	N Parrish	0.000	3		0	0	1	0
Mathematics 6	D Reeves	0.000	3		0	1	0	4
Social Studies 6	L Maclin	0.000	3		0	0	0	0
Reading 6	N Parrish	0.000	3		0	0	1	0
Band 6 - 180	R Holman	0.000	3		1	1	2	1
Science 6	L Hanna	0.000	3		3	0	3	1

```
Condct = Conduct          1 - Excellent       2 - Satisfactory
                          3 - Needs Improvmnt  4 - Unsatisfactory
```

Course	Comments
Mathematics 6	Ineligible for athletics unless passing 5 or more courses
Social Studies 6	Making no attempt to pass this course
Science 6	Inattentiveness in class/poor class participation

Middle School Report Card

11

South Side High

School Year: 2004-2005

1880 Prospect Memphis, Tennessee 38106 Ph.: 416-7380

Date Printed: 5/24/05

Gatewood, Eugene Lucious

Grade: 09
Homeroom: 04
Cumulative Credits: 5.00
Cumulative GPA: 1.000
Promotion Status:

Semester 1

Subject	Teacher	1st 6 Weeks Grade	Cond	Abs	Tar	2nd 6 Weeks Grade	Cond	Abs	Tar	3rd 6 Weeks Grade	Cond	Abs	Tar	Sem 1 Exam	Sem 1 Grade
GPA:		1.500				1.333				1.167					1.333
HOMEROOM 09	P. McKinney														
Family & Consumer Sc	M. Buford	76	S	0	3	78	S	0	0	80	N	0	1	85	78
English I	P. McKinney	63	N	2	0	77	S	3	0	80	N	2	0	76	74
Algebra I	S. Walker	71	N	0	0	72	N	0	1	70	U	1	0	49	70
Physical Science	M. Gunn	78	S	1	0	80	S	1	1	70	N	0	0	62	71
Content Area Reading	P. McKinney	65	N	0	0	84	S	0	0	61	N	2	0	61	70
Lifetime Wellness	T. Wallace	95	S	0	0	73	S	0	0	70	N	1	0	75	77

Semester 2

Subject	4th 6 Weeks Grade	Cond	Abs	Tar	5th 6 Weeks Grade	Cond	Abs	Tar	6th 6 Weeks Grade	Cond	Abs	Tar	Sem 2 Exam	Sem 2 Grade	Year Grade	Credit
GPA:	0.667				0.667				2.333					0.667		
Family & Consumer Sc	65	S	4	0	73	N	0	0	77	U	0	0	76	72	75	1.0
English I	71	N	5	0	72	N	3	0	77	S	2	0	39	68	76	1.0
Algebra I	70	S	9	1	69	U	9	1	73	S	0	0	60	72	71	1.0
Physical Science	70	N	9	0	70	N	1	0	74	N	0	0	58	70	71	1.0
Content Area Reading	73	N	8	0	72	N	0	0	100		0	0	55	74	71	1.0
Lifetime Wellness	0	S	5	0	0		0	0	100		0	0	100	0	0	0.0

Handwritten: 15-09-04 EUGENE L. GATEWOOD
PROMOTED TO GRADE 10 AT KIRBY HIGH
RETAINED IN GRADE ___ AT ___

Principal's Message:

High School Report Card

Parent's Signature _____

Conduct Legend: E - Excellent S - Satisfactory N - Needs Improvement U - Unsatisfactory

Grade Legend:
93 - 100 A
85 - 92 B
76 - 84 C
70 - 75 D
0 - 69 F
E Exempt
I Incomplete
N Not Applicable

Comment Legend:
1 - Excellent work and conduct.
2 - Continues to perform well in class.
3 - Has improved this six weeks.
4 - Keep up the good work.
5 - Has a positive attitude and good work habits.
6 - Does not complete homework and/or course requirements.
7 - Inappropriate and disruptive behavior.
8 - Excessive tardies to class.
9 - Unsatisfactory progress.
10 - Grades and attendance transferred from previous school.

12

If I Can Do It...
Anybody Can...

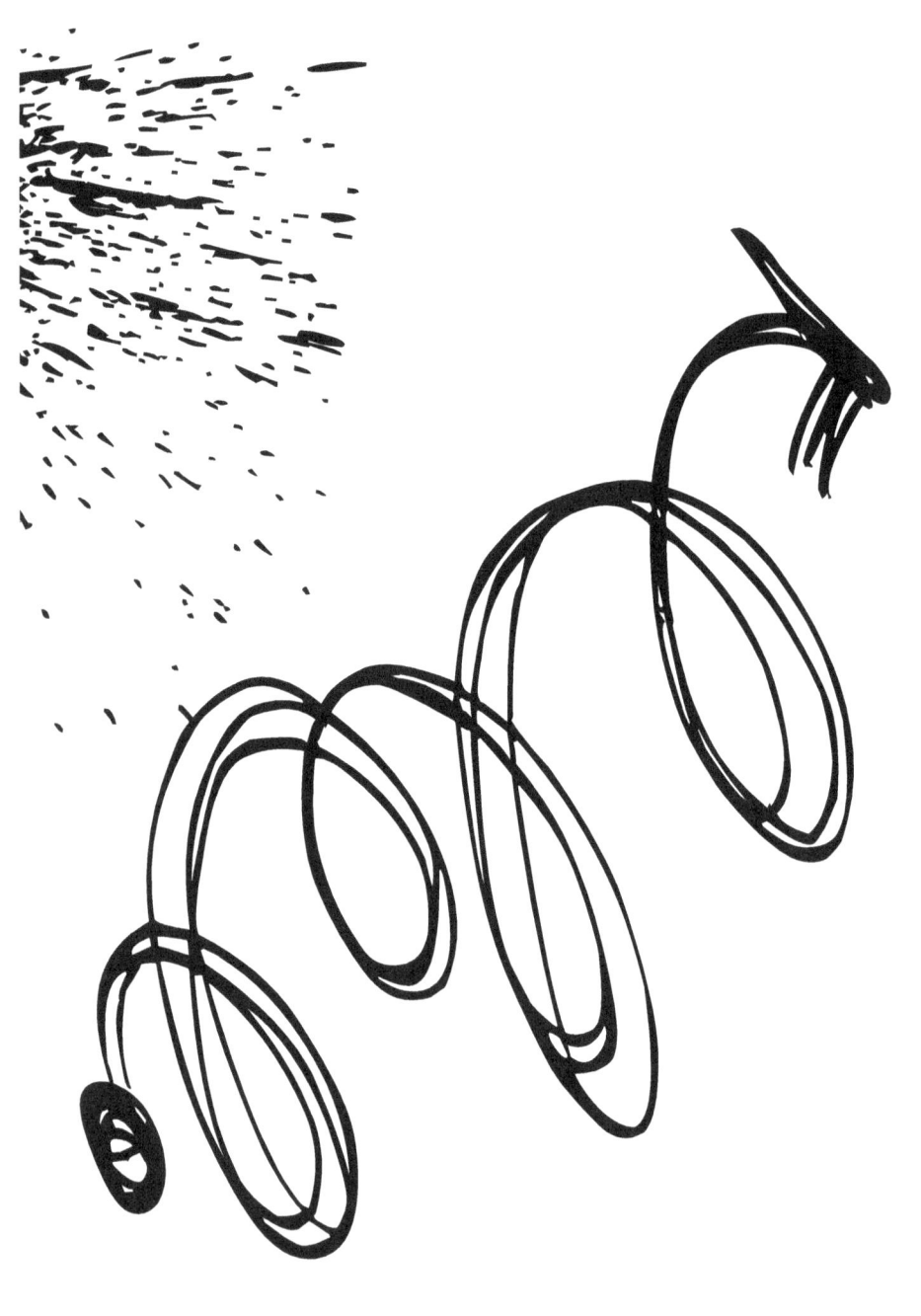

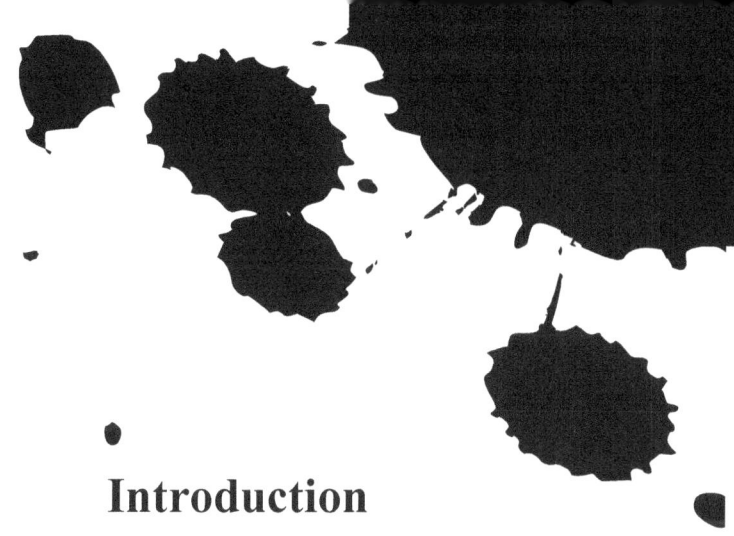

Introduction

I'm writing this book for US. This Ain't the watered down, This is the Real, The Uncut....

Anyone who knows me personally knows that I've always been kind of "crazy." Even when I was dead broke, dusty, sleeping on couches, and catching the bus, I always thought I was the biggest boss in Memphis and I couldn't be told differently. In my mind, the only people on my level were my idols like Master P, J Prince, Birdman, Dick Gregory, Malcolm X, Spike Lee, Snoop Dogg, and many others in that realm. Yes, I was very delusional back then, LOL. I never really followed anyone in my family because no one really ever did anything great, so I never had a great family blueprint to follow business wise. Don't get me wrong, my family is FULL of great, hard-working people who inspired me, helped me build my traits, my sense of humor, my pride, and my genetics, but I never got a blueprint for "independence" because nobody in my family was independent! Everyone in my family was either a worker, a hustler, or a leech. No one had businesses, No one was independent, nobody was self-made.

My biggest family inspirations are my mother and sister (two women). They both raised me since I was born and I watched them work every day of my life. My sister once worked three jobs at the same time, all while having a young child still in high school. So, excuses have NEVER been acceptable to us. They showed me how to work hard, be respectful, be grateful and how to LOVE, but I was never taught how to CREATE, BUILD or be THE OWNER. So, I started hustling and working early because I knew exactly what I wanted out of life. Not exactly HOW I would get it, but always had faith that I WOULD get it....

So, you should know I am writing this book, not as a mother fucker who's just talking, but from the point of view of someone who has actually done anything and everything imaginable to find different streams of income and make money. I've worked EVERY kind of job you can think of and tried every hustle under the sun, good, bad, legal, and illegal. From my first job at McDonalds when I was 16. From there, I worked at Popeyes Chicken to, Shoe Carnival, Nike Factory, to actual warehouses, over 50 plus Temporary Agency jobs, Carrier Air Conditioner, nursing homes as a CNA, several print shops, and over a dozen other odd jobs. Even while working those jobs, I always had the **MINDSET (**Chapter 1) that each job was just a steppingstone, and I would always find my way out. Maybe that's why I never stayed in one spot long. My longest job was for 3 years (wage was 22$ in 2012) which I left to go back to school for 0$, but we'll get into that in Chapter 4 (**The DOING**). So just know, when I say "Employee to Entrepreneur," Not only was I an employee, but I was THE EMPLOYEE! Staying late and coming early, walking, and riding the bus, offering to volunteer, always going above & beyond, bringing donuts to the office, winning countless Employee of the Month awards, and ready to break my back just for the opportunity to be seen by the company! (I *even rode my bike 9.2 miles from Yale Rd to Germantown Pkwy when I worked at Danvers for $11 hour in 2008.*) My sister and I still laugh every time I tell the story because the trip gets longer and longer every time I tell it, LOL.

I can speak about the Mindset of a worker because I was the ULTIMATE Worker before I became the Boss. I've always had the mentality of ownership and independence. The only difference now is that I work for myself. I apply that same work ethic I had then but now it's applied to MY WORK, and my work directly benefits me and my family's future.

But before making the decision of if you want to become an entrepreneur, first you must decide "WHY" you want to become an entrepreneur? Do you have a groundbreaking idea that will change the world? Do you provide a service you know that people need? Do you have a skill or talent that you know people will love? Is it because entrepreneurship looks like easy money or are you just lazy and don't want to go to work every day? Always remember, An entrepreneur wants more freedom not more Money. There are GREAT paying jobs out there that can provide all the money you can dream of, so don't ever think jobs can't get you where you need to go financially. A job can provide a security blanket that the unpredictable wages and sleepless nights that come with entrepreneurship don't. So, you must decide on what do you want. Are you OK with the 9-5 lifestyle? Are you living comfortably? Are your bills paid? Can you eat out a couple of nights a week? Can you go shopping pretty much whenever you feel the urge? Can you occasionally take off and go on vacation when you want to?

For most Americans, this is all they want and it actually sounds like a great life if your pay at work is nice and your coworkers and boss all respect you. Then that's an awesome environment to be in. If that's the case, you should ride that gravy train until the wheels fall off and build up that 401k in the process!

But sadly, for most people, that is not the case. Most of us work dead end jobs that don't provide a decent living wage, insurance, or room to grow. Many of us are working check-to-check waiting on the next big break, while some unemployed people sit around praying to the "Job Gods" that never seems to come. The fact is that many of us really don't have either the knowledge, **The Plan** (Chapter 2), the access, or the credentials to find a better way of living. (And yes, I said US because I was in the same exact position.) So hopefully after reading this book, you'll unlock something in yourself to start shifting your perception of jobs, money, entrepreneurship and your definition of freedom. Thanks to God and a little information and confidence, I was able to change my mindset and change the trajectory of my life and my family's future for generations to come.

Enjoy

I had to Unlearn and Relearn to change my family's life.
-Ganelle Mitchell

CHAPTER ONE

Reconditioning your Mind, Replacing old ways of thinking with new Healthy Habits and ways of Thinking….

FIRST THING FIRST

In my 30 plus years of living I've come across, worked with, and have family members that are some of the most talented people in the world. I'm talking about a rare, one-of-a-kind, raw ability that no one else is born with. Not like a skill that you can learn along the way, but a God-given natural talent. Some people aren't even aware of their gift because they've never been in an atmosphere to unlock it, or it was never discovered or nurtured as a child. Think about all the super talented people you know on your Job, in your family, or at your church with absolutely nothing to show for that ability or talent. (Take your time.) Now, take that same time and think about all the people you know or have come across with ZERO TALENT or no natural ability, but they are "insanely successful." Your boss, company owners, entertainers, public figures, and so on, Think about It! We might think it's *unfair* or they've gotten lucky. Maybe so, but most of the time, there's a key difference between the two people and that is their Mindset. The Mindset is the direct difference between a **Boss** and a **Worker**! And the HIGHLY successful people are often both.

A talented person without the proper mindset will think to themselves, "I need money so I need a job," instead of thinking, "I need money so how can I use my talent to generate revenue."

Two different outlooks to the same problem: MINDSET! Get the idea of JOB = MONEY out of your head NOW!

That is 100% not how it works, M*y whole family worked all their lives* and *ain't none of us got no damn money, LOL*! I've worked 100s of jobs and I didn't actually start getting money until I changed my Mindset and quit my Job. Until then, I lived month-to-month, day –to-day and check-to-check like 61% of all Americans.

So, stop thinking that just because you have a job you'll have money. The job should be looked at as a mutual partnership to help you get to where you eventually want to go. THAT'S IT! Now, where you ultimately want to go is your dream and whatever that dream is needs to be 100% clear so you know how to plan. Going through life without a plan is a pathway to nowhere. You'll look up and five years would've passed and you'll be at that same Job chasing a $4. raise. Have a Plan! With a clear plan and mindset, you go in knowing that the Job is just a part of the plan along the way. You pay me for my 40 work hours a week, while I use my other 128 hours to keep working on my plan. Business not Personal.

That's why you always see employees get emotional when a company fires someone or something shady happens to a longtime employee. They were so emotionally attached to the job and following the COMPANY PLAN, that they forgot to follow their *OWN PLAN*. The company plan is to pay you just enough where you have to keep coming back. Just enough to pay your bills and have a little fun but you eventually have to come back and keep coming back, day after day, week after week, year after year. At some point after 25 to 30 years, they'll pay you to leave. It's called retirement. You'll still get paid (Social Security), and the company keeps the wheel rolling with a new younger employee. All a part of the company plan. If you get sick and have to miss a day that's not part of the company plan, you'll be penalized. If your kids get sick and you have to leave work? Not the company's plan, You'll be docked pay. Want to take a week off for family vacation? Oh, HELL NO, we aren't paying you for that week. DEFINITELY not part of the company plan and you might not have a job when you get back, LOL! So, ditch the Mindset that the Job is there to save you. Their objective is to work you and pay you; nothing more, nothing less.

There are so many talented people stuck in the "WAREHOUSE "way of thinking. The "WAREHOUSE" way of thinking is, "I have a job and I get money. If I want more money, I work longer and harder on my job and I make more!" That is not how it works and if I thought that way, I would still be stuck at many of those same dead-end jobs that I worked.

So please don't let the Job = Money equation fool you.

Invest in yourself and you will Never Go Broke

Chase the Dream Not The Money

The Money should only be used as a tool, while what you DO with the money will decide your life.

• Money doesn't solve money problems.

• If you're ignorant with money winning the lottery wouldn't help. You'll just be back broke and ignorant in no time.

• Streams of income, a plan, resources, and tools are always better than Money!

"YOU" CONTROL YOUR TIME

• 168 Hours in a Week

• 40 Hour Work Week

• 128 Hours Left (for Rest, Family, Business, and Health)

• 40 Paid Hours

• 128 Unpaid Hours

What are you doing with your other **128 Hours**? Are you maximizing your time or are you just sitting back waiting for when it's time for you to go back to work?

 **Maximize your time.**

Discovering your Dream

Not the World's Dream or the American Dream, Your Dream!

Now this part is all on you. You decide what your dream looks like. Only you can see what your ending looks like. Some people want a billion dollars and a private island. Some people dream of a big family with lots of land to pass down for generations. Your end might be retiring from your company after 30 years with a six-figure 401k and investment properties. Some might just want to sit back and travel the United States in a RV. At the end of the day, it's you, and only you, who decides what that vision looks like.

Don't measure success or happiness by what you see. Measure it only by what you feel. Your definition of success might not be the same as everyone else's. To some, Rich equals successful. To some, Health is a form of success. My Mindset is, "As long as I don't have to ask anyone for anything and my family is comfortable, then I'm successful." Not filthy rich, but comfortable, that's all I want. What do you want? ***(Ask Yourself.)***

DREAM DISCOVERY WORKSHEET

Take your time and Be Specific with your Answers
Everyones Dream will be Different

1. What is your #1 Dream?

2. What is your Dream Job?

3. Why do you want to be an Entrepreneur?

4. How many Cars & Houses will you own?

5. Where is your Retirement Location?

Everyones Dreams are Different
EMBRACE THAT DIFFERENCE

Someone who knows what they want out of life also knows exactly what atmosphere they want and need to be in to create that environment for themselves. If I want to be a doctor but I'm in an environment full of plumbers, then I'm out of place. If I want to be a lawyer and I'm surrounded by cosmetologists, then obviously I'm in the wrong area. We have a saying in Memphis that goes, *"Catch Up with your Kind,"* meaning, "Go hang around what you are." Fish swim with fish, Bosses mingle with Bosses, workers hang with workers, and Entrepreneurs learn from Entrepreneurs. So, make sure you are always in the right places around the right people.

After my mindset shift, I had a dream of starting a print shop because I had the skills and a little talent in that area. I didn't have any money, but I had a Plan. My plan was to get a Job at a printshop to get in the environment I eventually wanted to own. I would learn everything I could about every aspect and detail of the business and save every dollar they gave me to **invest** back in my own business. I did that for 3 years at 4 different shops and became an expert in the field, all while collecting checks in the process of building my own shop. Can't beat it!

There's nothing wrong with working a Job when you:

A. Know **"WHY"** you're working the Job!

B. Understand how to "**WORK**" the Job!

C. Learn how to work your way "**OFF**" the Job!

The job should always be beneficial to you and should compliment your visions and life goals. If you want to be a dentist, get a job in a dental office. If you are an aspiring teacher, find a job at a school or work with a youth program. If you want to open a restaurant one day, start working at some local restaurants to see how things work and learn the language. If you want to start a business in a certain industry, find work within that industry early to get a head start. Even if it's for free. Volunteer work and internships are some great ways to get in some doors and start working within your vision. Just make sure you do whatever you can to get into the room. Don't underestimate the value of being in the right room around the right people. So, look for work that will help you on your path to achieving your dream. Don't just sell your 40 hours a week to anyone. It sounds more complicated than it actually is, but it comes back to the old saying from Confucius...

Choose a job you love and you never have to work a day in your life. -Kong Qiu

DREAM JOB?

What would be your dream job?

Think about this....

After a long day at work, do you feel like the work you've done has made a difference in your life or on someone else's life?

Is it a building block or a steppingstone to where you are trying to get to?

Is the work you're doing educating you or helping you become what you eventually want to become?

Or are you just selling them 40 hours of your time for that week?

Unlearn & Relearn

The key factor in advancing in life is what all we know. Knowing is Knowledge & Information is Gold, and those with the information have the Gold. PERIOD! What we know and don't know will have a bigger impact on our lives than any amount of money we could ever have in the bank. If someone had told me information and resources are a million times more valuable than money, I would have been at the library like it was a crack house.

As I got older, I realized I had to unlearn a lot of things I learned in school and in life. This was either because the information was untrue, unneeded, or I simply forgot about it to make room for new fulfilling information that would help me grow. School teaches us how to be a good employee but doesn't necessarily tell us how to be great business owners or how to make money on our own. School teaches workmanship not entrepreneurship. Math teaches us how to add, subtract, multiple, and divide the money but not the accumulation or the actual management of the money. The lies they taught us in Social Studies are laughable and to some cultures flat out disrespectful and 100% false. But In school, we were never taught to fact check or to DYOR! (Do Your Own Research). So, we just went along with the information given to get the passing grade. Participating in the *"ACT"* of learning, not ACTUALLY learning. They teach you that failing is wrong, but in life failing teaches us some of the most valuable lessons and teachers don't usually teach that.

Most of the information I learned that changed my life came from living life. I learned from the Earth and the wise and intelligent people that I was blessed to cross paths with! When I was 17, I worked part-time at my Aunt Sherri's (**Rest in Peace**) corner store. There was a barbershop next door. That is where I first meet the two men who would shape the rest of my life. Mr. Ray, the shop owner, and Terry G, the shop manager, were the first positive male influences I had in real life. Not someone on TV or a rapper, but real-life Men. This was not only because of what they showed me, but because of what they taught me. At the time, I was young, dumb, lost, and "street poisoned." I thought I knew everything but didn't know a damn thing. Mr. Ray, a Black businessman, entrepreneur, retired "player" was a well-dressed, self-made person straight from North Memphis. He had a gold painted pinky nail like a trophy for his 25 years plus **Staying Down** *(Staying true and consistent)* in the Game. He taught me tons about business, the old laws of the game, gentlemenship, consistency and manhood! The same with Mr. Terry, a black nationalist Master Barber and preacher, taught me how to be respectful and to be worthy of respect, and how to love and show love! He bought me my first real suit; a $700 suit from Joseph A Banks that I still have in rotation today. He treated me like a son he never had. Me not having a father in the house, I never learned, or was not exposed to certain things up close.

My only male influences came from TV or one of my sister's cool boyfriends. So, seeing Mr. Ray and Terry G was like seeing superheroes in person. I hung on their every word like it was the Bible. They treated me as an equal, kept everything upfront, and showed me respect that I had to earn from "staying down." The foundation of everything I know came from that shop. I had to unlearn all the poisonous bullshit I had learned to even understand the information, knowledge, and instructions I was being given every day. I was there every day like a fly on the wall sponging up the information and wisdom from age 17 until literally right now. I developed a healthy Mindset and learned how to be a Man before anything. I found my sanctuary, my study hall, my library, and my knowledge fountain, and it was not in a school. I had to find mine, now go find yours!

Intelligence vs Wisdom

KNOW THE DIFFERENCE

Intelligence is *what* you know and the ability to apply or communicate what you know.

Wisdom is the quality of having experience, knowledge, and good judgment.

Unlearn any bad habits, feelings, or any inappropriate or inaccurate information stuck in your mind. Old ways of thinking and doing things can be replaced by new ways of thinking and doing things. It all starts with the recognizing that change is possible and necessary for the personal growth and development of a healthy mindset. Fact check and DYOR on some of the key information you've been given throughout life. You may be surprised by what you discover. The way you feel or think about something Now might be different than you thought about it 10 years ago or maybe even one year ago. So, get that old, outdated crap out of your mind and make room for what can help and benefit your mindset now!

Relearn new innovative ways to see the world! Open your mind to new and diverse ways of thinking. Not just the traditional school ways of learning but through traveling and collaborations with wise and intelligent people. Once you open your Mindset, you'll open yourself up to more information than you'd ever imagine. And remember, that information is the Gold.

Train your Brain

Your Brain is Your Computer, You Decide What's Uploaded, Downloaded, Copied and Deleted. **CHOOSE WISELY.**

After a certain point in life, you're responsible for what you put into your body and mind. As children, we were taught what we were taught and learned what we were told to learn but as teenagers and adults, we have a choice. What information we put into our minds can affect us just as information files on a computer. The right file or program can make that computer move $1,000^x$ faster, and vice versa. A corrupted file can ruin an entire hard drive and kill the computer. The exact same thing is happening to our minds. Your brain is your computer, so you decide what's "Uploaded, Downloaded, Copied and Deleted." **CHOOSE WISELY**! Stop downloading useless material into your mind.

- You're either IN control, OUT of control, or UNDER control. -

Choose what you watch.

Choose what you listen to.

Choose what you surround yourself with.

Those factors are key in shifting yourself, your mindset, and changing the direction you want to go in life. So always be aware of what you're doing at all times. Start replacing unhealthy habits with productive habits. Ask yourself, is what I'm doing helping or hurting my mindset. Is what I'm watching teaching me anything useful or am I wasting brain space? Always be mindful of what you can be doing to help build towards your future. Even during your down time, can you be doing something to help your mindset develop? For example, instead of me sitting back smoking and watching The Simpson during my down time, I started watching episodes of Jeopardy instead. A slight shift, but it made a HUGE difference because even in chill mode, my brain was still working, and I was actually learning unconsciously during rest. Small replacements like that can make a big difference in the long run. So, think about what slight tweaks you could make on your path.

Challenge yourself:

Replace a bad habit with a healthy habit.

Replace your favorite album with your favorite podcast or audiobook.

Replace your favorite snack with your favorite fruit or vegetable.

Replace your favorite 30-minute show with a 30-minute educational video.

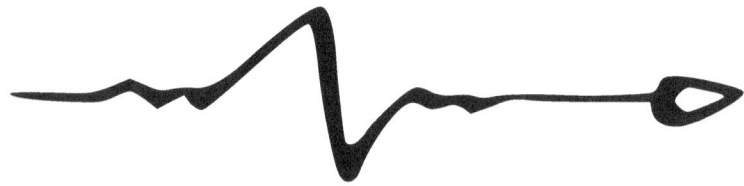

HABIT REPLACEMENT WORKSHEET

REPLACING OLD AND UNHEALTHY HABITS WITH PRODUCTIVE AND HEALTHIER HABITS

HABITS **RESULTS**

OLD HABIT	REPLACED HABIT	RESULT OF REPLACEMENT
Drinking Soda	Drinking Water	Cleaner system, More Energy
Eating Out	Cooking at Home	Saves Money, Healthier Food
Doing Drugs	Exercise	Feel Better, Live Longer

SOME CHANGES WILL BE *BIG* AND SOME WILL BE *small...*
BUT EVERY CHANGE MATTERS!!!

It all sounds easy, but it takes a lot of **focus**, **self-control**, and **self-motivation**. These are habits that I've developed along the way over a span of 15+ years. Some days are easier than others and no day is perfect, but every day is an opportunity to grow and keep going. Just know, I will never tell anyone anything or speak about things I haven't personally done myself. So, when I talk about something, it's something I've done with my own two hands or a path I've traveled with my own two feet on the concrete. So, for sure if I can do it, it can be done. No Excuses, No Help, you've got to do it! You must go out and learn for yourself because that's where it starts, within.

FOCUS

Learn to *FOCUS*

Follow .**O**ne. **C**ourse. **U**ntil. **S**uccessful!

Learn when to have **laser** focus and when to have **lightbulb** focus.

Laser Focuses on only one thing, nothing else. It's true tunnel vision, a "no stopping till you get there" approach.

Lightbulb Focus is a broader vision, allowing you to put light on different things at once.

Both are needed at times, so learn to use them to your advantage.

Self-Control

You can't control anything or anyone if you're unable to control yourself. Self-control is one of the hardest things to master in the world. Learn ways to control your thoughts, your actions, and interactions. Self-control is like a superpower that makes people look wiser, smarter, and more disciplined than they might actually be. This might be for no other reason than they are in control of themselves and their emotions in every situation. The ability to say "no" when it's so easy and convenient to give in and say "yes" is an ability everyone should master over themselves.

Learn to Control Distractions and Self-distractions.
Don't let the world distract you and learn not to distract yourself. Don't take time out of your work and fill it with distractions. If you're studying and the phone rings, don't allow the distraction to deter you. If you're on social media for hours a day wasting brain space instead of filling those hours with productive activities, stop distracting yourself.
Distractions come in all shapes and forms. Be aware of what's trying to get your attention and make sure it's worth your time!

Don't be Distracted by the Distractions. - Elgen McFerren Jr.

Self-Motivation

Most of your time will be spent alone inside of your own head, so you should be your own main source of energy and motivation. No one should have to tell you that you're great before you tell yourself. No one should make you get up and be motivated every morning. You should wake up every day with a plan in mind and your brain should be working on a way to get that goal accomplished. Even on days where the energy level is low and you're not feeling your best, your brain should always be working. Speak life into yourself. Daily affirmations are great ways to stay self-motivated. Speak what you want into fruition by believing exactly what you say. Stand on the words that come out of your mouth proudly. You are your own cheerleader, so get those pom poms ready! Most of the time you'll be cheering alone, so you have to be the loudest and proudest. Like my business partner Proper Visions always said, *"You gotta wake up on it like you want it"*. It all starts with the mindset "**If you think it, you can do it**"**,** simple and plain. Everything in this world started with a thought, so don't think yours is crazy or impossible. I've got family members right now that if I told them I was writing a book they'll laugh at me and say, "Hell no, that's impossible," lol.

But look at this, **The Impossible....**

Those who believe they can, CAN!
Those that believe they can't, CANNOT!

- Charles Capps
(1934 - 2014)

CHAPTER TWO

Planning your work and Working your Plan. Leave no stone unturned and no idea undiscovered!

Proper Planning

Many of us know WHERE we want to be in life, but don't really know HOW we're going to get there. It takes strategy and consistency to maneuver through the ups and downs of life to become successful. One thing is for sure - two things for certain, we all want to be successful. There are two necessary steps to get there: Consistency and a proper Plan. Remember now, everyone's definition of success is different, so it's important for you to make your plan based on which direction you want your life to go in.

Do you plan on having a wonderful job and one day becoming the Boss of the company? Do you plan on building a recording studio and blowing up while traveling the world performing your music? Maybe it's just getting a little car wash or a laundry mat. You know, something that'll pay you recurring revenue every month without you having to show up? Pick one or *fuck it, do"em"all.* You can do whatever you want to do every day of the week if you make a plan and do the work to get it done. I've seen it all done, so I know it can be done.

Find what interests you! Find out what you're good at doing and find ways to monetize it! Everyone has a talent that no one else in the world possesses. You just have to find a way to tap into it or put yourself in the environment to unlock it. You might be thinking, "I don't have a special talent," or "I'm not good at anything." If that's what you're thinking, then go back to Chapter 1 and get your mindset together because I don't know what else to tell you.
You have to know your worth and know your worthy of everything you dream of. Discover that talent inside of you, and if not a natural talent then learn a skill and master it. There are many skills you can acquire that will get you paid and change your life and your families lives if you take the time to learn and master them.

I really don't have a natural born talent such as a painter like Aubrey Horton does, I'm not a great Musician like

Micheal Jackson was or a Lebron James who was just born a phenomenon. But I have a Full tool belt of skills that I've mastered and can cash in at any time. Surprisingly, some people acknowledge but neglect or even Hate their gifts. You ever heard a talented singer that says they hate singing, or an outstanding hair stylist that absolutely hates to do hair, or even a talented chef that hates cooking. It's total nonsense to me and more than likely these people are working jobs they hate instead of using that talent God gave them or skill they've learned as a steppingstone to build something greater. It doesn't have to be your end all be all, but your talent can be the head start you need in life. Wasted talent is the worst thing in the universe so please don't be that person that just takes up space on earth. Start with what interests you then build from there.

Master a skill by putting the time into it, putting your own unique twist on it so no one can do it quite like you. Write down your skills and the things you're talented at and think "could this benefit people as a product or service"? Find what you like doing and find a way to get paid for doing it.

LEVELS of the Game

1. **Interest** (you're interested in Something)

2. **Hobby** (your interest became a hobby, and you enjoy doing it)

3. **Skill** (your Hobby became a Skill that you are taking seriously)

4. **Pro** (Now you're getting paid from that Skill that you've learned)

5. **Master of the Game** (Now you've Mastered your Profession and No one can Do what you Do you) You become Tiger Woods, Micheal Jordan, Muhammad Ali, Bill Gates, Bruce Lee, a true Master!

MASTERING TAKES 10,000 HOURS

1 year 51 Days

LEARN / STUDY / DEVELOP / PRACTICE

Remember the Talent vs Skill comparison? Well, lets dig deeper....

Find the thing that comes the easiest to you and master it - Erika Badu

Talent vs Skill Analysis

The difference between talent and skills
Both can be monetized

TALENT

1. Talent is an inherent ability
of a person to do something
- Inborn Gifts
- You recognize your Talent
- Only a few people have that talent

SKILL

2. Skill is the expertise to
do a particular Thing effectively
- Developed gift
- You Develop your skill
- Anyone can learn & perfect that skill

TALENT
- Athelete
- Musician
- Dancer
- Artist
-
-
-

SKILL
- Doctor
- Lawyer
- HVAC
- Mechanic
-
-
-

ADD
THREE
EXAPMLES

Finding Your Lane

There are over a thousand different ways to make money. Cutting grass is one, babysitting is another, selling cars is another, and so on. So that leaves over 997 more ways to create sources of income. You just have to find your lane. Figuring out what side hustle or business works for you can be overwhelming at first, but if you follow this formula, it will become easier for you to figure out.

$$X + Y = Z$$

Use your *SKILL* or *talent* to create a *product* or a *service*.
(*Your* X)
Now take that **service** or **product** and ADD a *customer*.
(Your Y)
That equals *INCOME. (Your Z)*

**Now let's take a closer Look
to fully understand this Formula....**

THE BUSINESS MATHMATICAL FORMULA

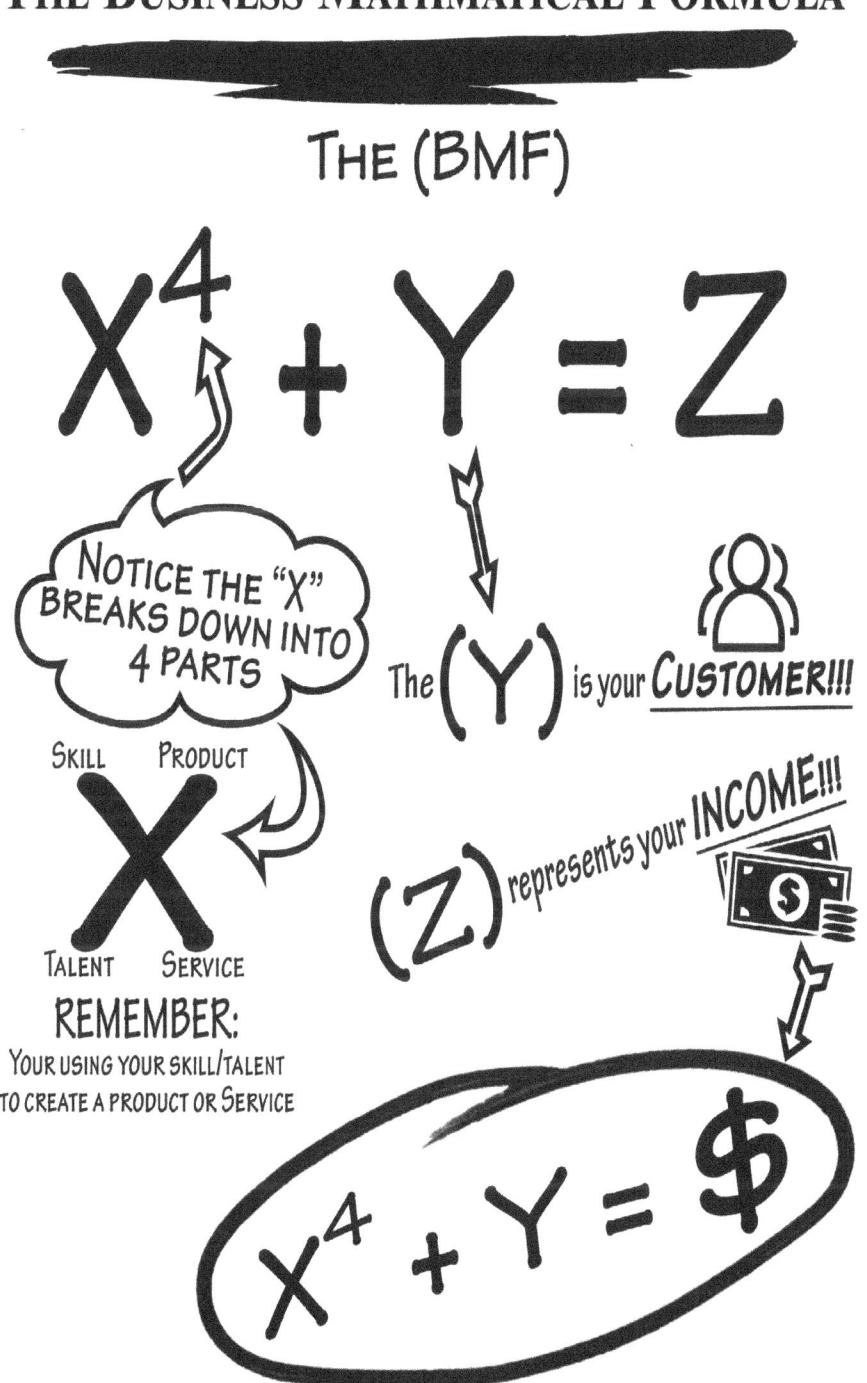

Types of Work

Body Work & Brain Work

There are two types of work; you can choose which fits you best. Body work and Brain work.

Body work is where you physically work to get paid. (Warehouse workers, Construction Worker, Fast Food employee, Police and Firemen, etc.)

Brain work is where you're working mentally to get paid. (Web Designer, Therapist, Architect, Marketing, Consulting, Fashion Designer, etc.)

Figure out what works for you and your skillset. Always remember *"Everything ain't for Everybody"* so find your lane.

The most powerful thing you can do is control what people see, hear, and eat.

A great business should provide 1 out of the 3

Self-Awareness

No matter what position you're in in life, being honest with yourself will always make every situation easier. Never put yourself in a position that you know your not ready for or your uncomfortable in. It will not go well for you at all and could cause you to lose time, money, and resources, and if you're not a strong-minded person you could potentially lose confidence and self-esteem. If you're not ready for a certain role or lifestyle sit back and groom yourself. Study and work extra hard to prepare yourself for what all comes with that lifestyle. Remember, their plate might look good and full until you have to eat it all and you realize your eyes were bigger than your stomach. So always be honest with yourself. Think about what you can do and what can't you do? Learn your strengths and weaknesses. What you're good at and need improvement on. Do what works for you, NOT THEM, but you....

It's just like planning a vacation, one person might plan the whole vacation the route, the hotels, food, and activities all at once weeks before they even leave their house. The other person might just cut on the GPS, hit the highway, and say "I'll figure it all out when I get there, or I can book the room on the way".
Same vacation, different trip.... Do what works for you!

ALWAYS FOLLOW THE NUMBERS

If something is working for you go for it. Keep rolling it until the wheels fall off, it'll help you in the long-term execute your plan. If you want to quit your job to start a clothing line but everyone knows you at your job for cooking great food. Maybe you should follow what's working for you and let the cooking be steppingstone to the clothing line. Don't overthink things or get in your own way. As business owners we try new crazy things instead of sticking to what got us successful. Instead, we think we must catch up or keep up with what's going on or overthinking trying to stay 5 steps ahead that we end up slowing down our progress by trying things that don't work instead of following the numbers to see what's already working. If I'm successful selling fruit and my top seller is grapes, and I haven't sold any oranges. Common sense would be I need to double up on the grape orders and slow down on oranges for a while. Follow what's working for you. You make more money from your job than you do doing photography, work the job and let the job income build your photography. Then when the time comes where your photography numbers surpass the job numbers then you can follow those numbers. Until then keep building and following the path that has been feeding you.

LISTEN TO YOU

Everything takes time and the times ahead of you are VERY HARD! The days are rough, and the nights are lonely. On this path you are your only support system so understand that now. I'm not saying no one cares about you as a person, but it's nobody's job to care about your dream when everyone has their own. So don't talk about it. *Go do it...*

Your plan is your plan, and everyone is not going to see it like you see it. Stop listening to negative people. Friends, family, coworkers or whoever, don't let that negativity affect you. I have family members that to this day tell me I don't have a real job. Sometimes they aren't even knowingly being negative or unsupportive, they just still have that employee's mindset. School, job, marriage, family, retirement, THATS IT! Their mindset might not even allow them to process the information or idea you're presenting to them, or they might not even know how to communicate well enough to respond to what their being told.

It's not their fault, it's their MINDSET. If an excited Bird runs up to tell a fish about a new idea to sell other Birds, their own nest. The fish would look at the bird like What the hell is a nest?..
It's not being harsh or dismissive it just truly not understanding the idea, or the information given. So don't

take offense to someone not seeing your vision or giving you the feedback you would want. Their mindset might just not understand your plan, it's your business and their opinion. That is it....

THE DOGS, CAT & RABBIT

There were two dogs, a cat, and a rabbit, who all live on the same street!

The dog had a brilliant idea to sell fire hydrants to other dogs in the neighborhood!

He told the rabbit and the rabbit said that was an awesome idea!

So now he was **EXCITED** about his plan!

He ran and told the cat! The cat didn't say anything because he didn't even know what a fire hydrant was because he was a cat.

So now he was **UNSURE** about his plan!

He walked over and told the other dog! The dog told him that would be a stupid idea and laughed.

So now he was **DISCOURAGED** about his plan!

So he ran home sad and sat in the house for two weeks depressed and second guessing his idea.

One day he finally decides to go back outside and all of a sudden, he sees fire hydrants lined up down the street. He asked the cat and rabbit what was going on and they told him to ask the other dog!

As he walks up, the other dogs shouts out with a handful of money "*your stupid idea actually worked*"!

The moral of the story is "**STOP LISTENING TO FOLKS**"! Don't take advice from everybody. Advice is cool if it's from someone who has played the game. If you're a Towel boy and you're trying to tell me how to coach my team "go take a nap"! I know in life you can learn anything from anyone at any time. A homeless man on the street can give you wisdom, but when it comes to your business watch what advice you follow and stop listening to every damn body! What works for them might not work for you!!

Always Remember: Nothing ever goes 100% according to your plan that's why it's important to have a Plan B and go all the way down to at least Plan P. I know a lot of people say if you have a plan B you not 100% in plan A. But sometimes, having a backup plan can be the difference between success and failure. Nothing goes right 100% of the time, that's why cars have seatbelts, Plan B, and if the seatbelt doesn't work, they've even added a Plan C which are the airbags. Lol. Always protect your future with forward thinking. Always be 365 moves ahead so you're never caught by surprise. It's been times my Plan D saved my life so always Plan ahead and put your all in every Plan you have.

Plan your work and work your plan! A to P - 1 to 16!

Leave no stone unturned or idea undiscovered

Think x Outline x Attack

You might not be able to do all you find out, but you should

find out all you can do... - Jim Rohn

(1930 - 2009)

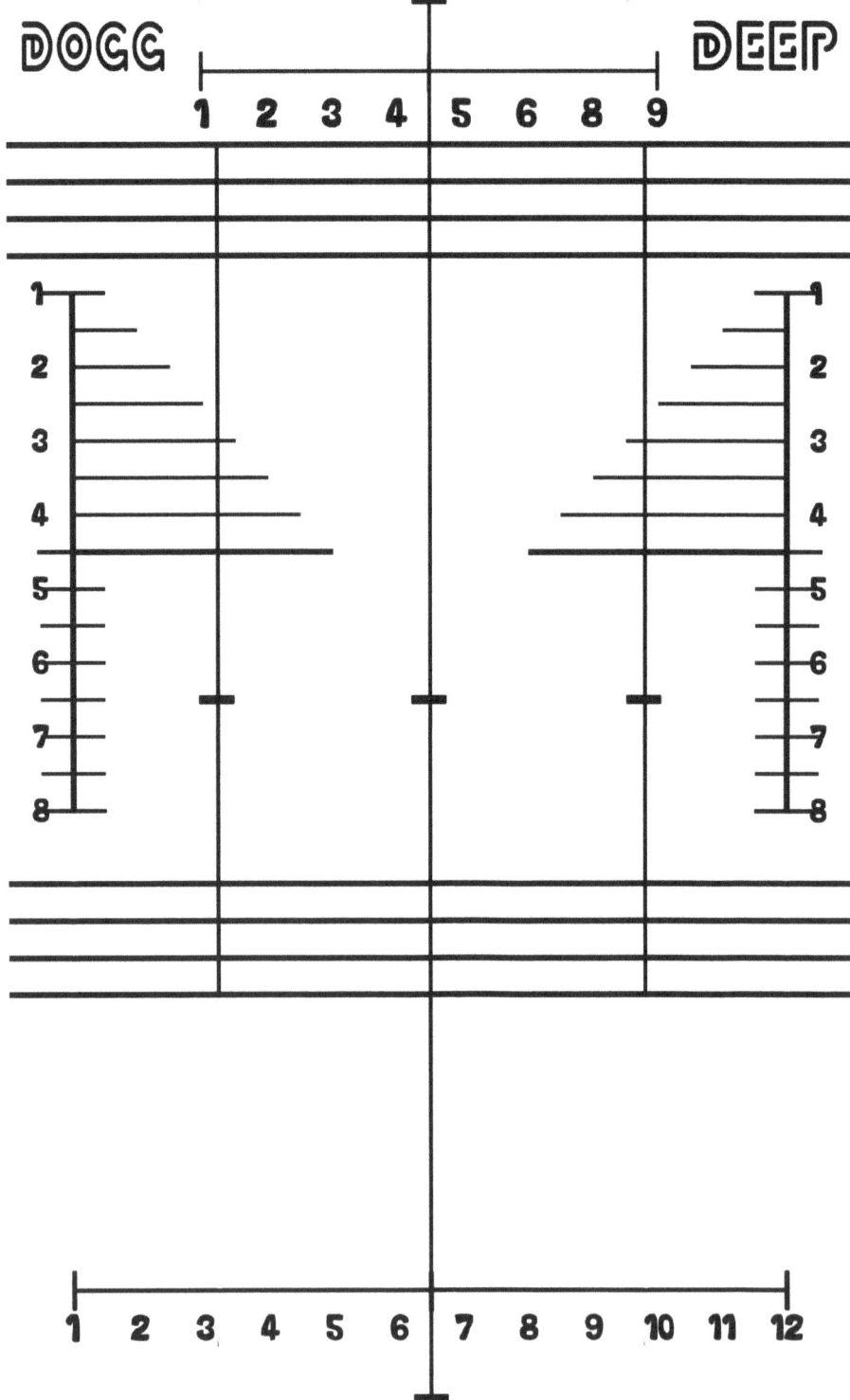

CHAPTER THREE

The base on which everything strong stands...

BUILD STRONG

Build a foundation that's strong and that will stand firm in the hard and rocky times ahead! The stronger the mindset and the stronger belief in the plan, the stronger the foundation will become. Build something that's based on hard work, honesty, loyalty, and accountability. These core values will take you and your business a long way.

-Hard Work

Start building your foundation by doing the hard work necessary to be successful. No shortcuts, No Handouts, No Cheat Codes, you have to do the work. You can tell the difference between someone who's worked hard for what they've gotten in life vs someone who has just been handed the keys or took the easy way up. Their values and work ethic will be different. The appreciation for the process will be different from a person who took the elevator up compared to us who've taken the stairs. Hard work instills pride in the business and gives it character in the community. The village respects an owner from the village because they've seen the hours and years they've put into the business and that makes them feel like they're apart of the growth. Community and hard work is key to a strong Foundation. A hard worker is always respected in life and in business. And as the boss you have to be the hardest worker in the building. So, roll up your sleeves and get to work!

-Honesty

Honesty is one of the most respected qualities in life and in business. People might not like always hearing the truth, but they will respect you for keeping it real. And it gives them an option to deal with you or not. Me personally, I love doing transparent business, either as the worker or the boss in the situation. Let me know exactly where we stand, let me know my true position so I know exactly how I need to work it, so it can work for me. As a business, always keep it real with your employees and customers. If you run an honest operation, you'll forever have a loyal base. Total transparency and being up front with your customers and partners builds the trust needed to make a 1-time deal become a lifelong partnership.

-Loyalty

Be loyal to your business, your customers, and your community. Be a service to those who are a service to you. "People over pennies" is a phrase I heard young, and it stuck with me like a mother fucker because I knew that's exactly how I was going to run my business. People First. Your customers are a blessing and to *SEE* a blessing you have to *BE* a blessing. Learn your people, learn your environment, and give back to who gave to you when you feel the need, and watch how it will make a difference in your future and in your business's future.

-Accountability

Hold yourself accountable and the others around you! Eliminate all yes men in your corner because they will only watch you fail. Embrace the criticism and the tough love, it is needed and respected in business and in life. Learn when it's time to pat yourself on the back and when it's time to kick yourself in the ass. It'll be plenty of time for both but you have to set the tone for what kind of operation you want to run. When you make excuses, you get an excuse-based operation. When you crush deadlines and get the job done no matter what, you get a no nonsense operation. When you hold yourself up to a certain standard people notice and that becomes the standard. So don't make excuses or find other people to blame for when things are going wrong. Take full accountability and responsibility when things go wrong so when things go right, you'll get the full credit.

YOUR IDENTITY

The foundation of any good company is based on the foundation and principles of its owner. Your business will be ran how your life is ran. Your reputation is your business's reputation. Sometimes unfair but it is what it is. That's why some people own faceless companies where the owner is completely unknown because they understand that their personal reputation could potentially hurt their business's success. So always be aware of your personal Identity because a slick and slimy owner will own and operate a slick and slimy business. No way around it!

Never act like "The Boss" instead of an employee. An entrepreneur is EVERYTHING AT ALL TIMES, so you have to be everything at all times.

I've seen bosses lose great employees and ruin whole companies and personal relationships trying to be just "THE BOSS." Never think you're too big to do the work. Never use the phrase "I don't know how." You automatically expose your weaknesses. Instead, you can just say "I haven't learned that yet" it shows that you're at least open and willing to learn what you don't know. Never expect others to do what you won't do or what you haven't taken the time to learn. ***Stop Being Lazy***! People will see that and start to resent you for it and that could lead to a bad reputation or even unhappy employees sabotaging your business from the inside. Every solid foundation has a strong backbone it can lean on, so you have to be prepared to play every position needed to stand strong. Even if you have to stand alone...

The world is Buyer Beware instead of Seller be Honest -

Dick Gregory
(1932 - 2017)

Everything
Ain't
For
Everybody

-Jermaine Shute

The Two Toung theory

The Toung on your shoes and the Toung in your mouth should do the same thing…

Lamest terms: *WALK IT HOW YOU TALK IT*

Dumber terms: *SAY WHAT U MEAN*

APPEARANCE

Now this part is a double-edged sword because I've been on both sides and can see both arguments on appearance. On one hand the suit and tie business look demands respect and makes you seem smarter and more sophisticated than we might actually be. And like my partner Sheldon Davis (a serial entrepreneur) said to me once *"you never know whose hand you might have to shake today so always look presentable."* On the other hand, now days you see the super casual t-shirt sweatpants flip flop wearing Multi Multi Millionaire that might not look to part at first sight but once they start talking you understand 100% why they're Multi Multi. Example Dallas Cowboy owner Jerry Jones vs Dallas Maverick owner Mark Cubin (DYOR) It's really based on your preference and what makes you comfortable but always remember the world will judge you so make sure your ducks are in a row and you know the language because you will be challenged based on your looks. If you carry yourself a certain way you will have to back it up at some point, so make sure your so good they can't fuck with you no matter how your hair looks or how you dress, gender, or race. Always remember, *the way I dress didn't get me in the room, the way I think did!*

THE POWER OF NETWORKING

Now this part is one of the most important parts of the book. So let us slow down and get your highlighters ready.

As an entrepreneur every time you leave the house it's an opportunity for you to get paid. Everywhere we go is a potential business meeting, an advertising opportunity, or a potential new vendor relationship. Let's get deeper, every contact in your phone is a potential customer you already know. Every coworker at your job is a potential client or a test dummy for your new product. Every member of your church is a potential testimonial for the service you provide. There is a person you went to school with that's in the exact field you're trying to get into and they're ready and willing to share the information with you, but you don't even have each others numbers. The customer base you want is already there, just get out there and network. You'll be surprised who is actually looking for exactly what you have to offer, they just don't know you have it.

My partner Elgen has a strategy that every time he goes into a store with long lines, he uses that as a networking and promotional opportunity. Instead of getting mad or impatient about 50 people in front of him in line, he sees that as 50 potential customers in front of him. Set some time aside specifically for networking time. It can be 1 hour a week to start, but you most definitely have to start. You can start with your social media; the internet has an unlimited amount of people you can reach. Take 30 minutes a day to promote your business and engage with customers on social media a day. Join groups with likeminded individuals and people in your field of interest. Get out and hand out business cards every Wednesday. Get out there and network, let it be know what all services you provide.Your family, your friends, your coworkers, everyone who knows you should know exactly what you do and know how to always contact you. 75% of my business comes from word of mouth to this day!

You will get most of your business through the relationships you build during the process. A stranger will support your business faster than a person you've known from the sandbox, so get out there and meet the world and build your contact list. It is the most valuable thing you have in this Game.

- "What you know and who you know will 100% determine where you go!" -

RESOURCES OVER MONEY

Notice I said your contact list is the most valuable thing you have, **Not Money!** That's because the right contact is worth more than any dollar amount. Relationships build your resources, and resources are way more valuable than money. I've been in rooms where any amount of money couldn't get me in the room it took relationships. I've been given some of the biggest opportunities in my life through referrals from my contact list. I used to pay thousands of dollars to go to see the Memphis Grizzlies games, now I literally have a relationship with the arena where I can walk in anytime I want to go sit front row every game if I wanted to. The relationship became a resource, and that access is a resource money can't buy.

Another example, I bought a house, and the AC unit was busted. Instead of having to call around and wait in the 100-degree weather for someone to show up, I automatically went to my contact list and called one of my brothers Mike Burkett who owns a HVAC company (Major League Mechanical). He showed up, fixed the unit, and actually **REFUSED** to let me pay a dollar. Real brother, real relationship, and real resource. In every industry I know an owner, every one of my close friends and mentors owns a business.

If I need a vehicle (Roger Auto Business) if I need tires for that vehicle (Mario's Tire Shop). If I'm hungry I can't call the owner of McDonalds, but I know several restaurants and food truck owners I do business with I can call. Like the saying goes "*There's power in proximity*" so build your resources. I love building resources and being a resource to my people. They know they can call me anytime for my print company, or film work or if they need me for marketing, website work, advice, or whatever resource I have to offer. I'm spoiled to the point where I don't want to go outside of my circle for anything and really if you build a strong contract list with strong relationships you shouldn't have to. Get out there, network, hit the internet, find local events, and pop out. "Go put your feet on the concrete and put some numbers in your phone."

I met one of my best friends, my brother Jack Simon on Eventbrite at his free "Event planning workshop" he organized in 2012 and the rest was history. He taught me everything he knows, and he has access to everything I have. My right-hand man and late brother James Mitchell was the king of using your resource and relationships. We literally mastered the game and went undefeated for over a decade. Team building, relationship building, state to state, cross country doing the work, learning the work, and building the resources. He would always say **"Gone finish the book P,** *they need to hear this shit, Mane."* So, this is why I'm saying that this is the most important part of the book, because my relationships and my resources got me everything I have today, not the money. *Money can't buy what I Got!*

If we ain't got no BUSINESS Together, then we ain't got no business together.... Entreprener Proverb

Learn the Power of Networking
BUILD YOUR AUDIENCE (all outlets)

Social media and real life, people you know and strangers .

Here's an example of some foundation building habits you can use and feel free to add a couple of your own techniques that you think would be helpful to your building.

THE FOUNDATION BUILDING CHECKLIST

BE HONEST WITH YOURSELF.

DON'T ANSWER "YES" WHEN THE ANSWER IS "NO"

IF YOUR "ALMOST THERE" THAT'S FINE

YOU'RE ON YOUR WAY

BUT NEVER GET COMFORTABLE WITH "ALMOST"!!

	YES	NO	ALMOST THERE
ONE HOUR OF READING A DAY	☐	☐	☐
FOUR SOCIAL MEDIA POST A WEEK	☐	☐	☐
HAND OUT 200 BUSINESS CARDS A MONTH	☐	☐	☐
_____	☐	☐	☐
_____	☐	☐	☐
_____	☐	☐	☐
_____	☐	☐	☐
_____	☐	☐	☐
_____	☐	☐	☐

So, to end this chapter I'll leave you with this. Make sure you have a solid FOUNDATION built on faith. Your faith doesn't necessarily mean religion, but you must put your faith in something. It can be GOD, it can be the universe, you can put your faith in your family, or having faith in your future plans can be a great motivative factor. But always have faith and believe in what you're doing and what you can do. Faith builds a strong Foundation. So, get out there and mix and mingle, build your contacts, use the people you already know for practice so when it's time to go show the world your talent you're ready and confident. Keep building and networking with your peers and find different ways to get yourself discovered. Rely on the resources, contacts, and connections you've gained for help and advice, and be available to them in their time of need!!! That builds the strongest relationship and a strong Foundation. Live your life respectfully and build your Foundation on faith and your business will grow gracefully and organically.

You have to meet

ALL CHALLENGES in life

BIG or small

Because how you start is How you finish
- **Bernie Mac**
(1957 - 2008)

76

CHAPTER FOUR

The CHOICE

Make the choice to take a Chance...

Chances & Choices

Many people come up with some of the best and most brilliant ideas, but they never came to fruition because they've never had the confidence to take a chance. If you have an idea without a proper plan to bring that idea to reality, then you're just dreaming and after a while, you'll wake up from that dream broke saying I could've, would've and should've instead of saying, "I did it or at least I tried". Even if you fail you have to try. Some people are so scared of not succeeding or losing that they never get in the game, they sit on the sideline and watch everyone else play the game. Some people even have the audacity to ridicule other people for losing when they never even participated or tried to accomplish anything themselves, these are the worst kind of people. If you have a good idea or something you believe will benefit the world, get it out of your head and give it to the world! Make the choice and take a chance.

There are 7 days in a week

Someday and Oneday are NOT ONE OF THEM!

If you feel it and you know it will work bust your move. Go with your gut feeling. Just like Richard Montanez, the son of Mexican immigrants. He was the janitor at the Frito Lay warehouse when he came up with the idea of Flamin' Hot Cheetos. He knew that his community loved the flavor and if given the chance the world would too. So, he busted his move and went over the manager and supervisor's head and called the owner directly to give him the idea and a sample of the recipe, and the rest is history. Flamin' Hot is one of the most popular flavors in the world, and it was all possible because he said fuck it and took his chance. Don't sit back thinking "What If?" You have to take a chance to advance, and always remember the bigger the risk the greater the reward.

You can't Fail until you Quit.... Starlito

Fear

The 3 biggest fears we have as humans is the fear of death, the fear of failure, and fear of poverty. These fears are often the reason most people never take a chance at anything. Those fears breed doubt, and that doubt limits the choices that you will ultimately make in life. Some people go through life doing things that they really don't want to do because they feel like they don't have a choice. Just like many people have let time pass them by and looked back kicking themselves in the ass because they've never taken a chance on anything they loved. I know that exact feeling, I had the opportunity to go on tour with some of the biggest upcoming performers in the music industry in 2012 for some video work, instead I turned it down because I had to be at work that week and couldn't afford to take off. Those artists have gone on to become multi-platinum selling Grammy nominated artist and I missed a *KEY* potential life shifting opportunity because I was scared to bet on myself and take a chance.

To this day that is still one of my biggest regrets, because instead of taking a chance on myself I made the easy choice and went to work. I've had countless jobs since then but NEVER got an opportunity quite like that one since then. That missed opportunity lit a fire in me and from that point on I said no matter what I have to do, no matter how much money I have or don't have. I'm betting on myself every time. If you have to put your faith in anything, why not put it in yourself? I swear to God after that moment I said *Never Again*! Never again will I not take a chance on myself, and I made a choice. I put in my 2-week notice enrolled in college and never looked back.

I swore to myself that I was going to create a bigger opportunity for myself than the one I fucked up. I had already at that point maxed out at that Job in only 3 years at $22 an hour and I had already been following my plan. The first year at the job I invested in all studio equipment and started a small recording studio. My second year at the job I bought all video equipment and start doing photography and shooting music videos which gave me the chance to go on that tour which I didn't take. And the third year I bought screen printing equipment and started my printing company from scratch. So, by the time I made the choice that it was time to leave I had already invested in my tools, which I paid for with the money I made from the job. I had an audience and contacts list who were mostly the people I worked with every day. So instead of getting stuck at the Job I stuck to my plan and worked my way "**OFF**" the job. I went to school for graphic design and during that time I built a bigger audience and contact list, so by the time I graduated my resources were plentiful and my foundation was built.

I took a chance that changed my life, and it was one of the scariest decisions I've had to make. Leaving a good paying job everyone in my family said I was a damn fool. What kind of job will Graphic Design get you? That's not a *real job*. I heard it all and went through it all. I made my choice and took a chance, and that decision changed my life forever. I've had both the $10 dollar month and the $10,000 months but if you made it this far through the book then you know that it's two sides to entrepreneurship. Before you make your choice, Decide are you choosing money or freedom? I didn't leave the job because I needed more money, the money was GREAT, I left because I needed my freedom.

Make your Choice.

Your making the **Choice** that:
"This is what I'm meant to do and whatever path I have to take will be 100% worth it because I've prepared for this moment"!

(repeat daily)

Your making the decision and having faith and
confidence in your plan.

Stand on It!

SACRIFICE

Freedom takes sacrifice. Remember you're making your choices based on freedom not money. If you do what you're supposed to do and live your life right, you'll be blessed with riches beyond your imagination. So don't ever make a decision based on just the money, or you will be back in that employee mentality instead of making a decision based on your future goals, and the future you want will take some sacrifice. So always think ahead. Not for today but tomorrow and beyond. Like I said, I bought equipment each year just to set up things that I could monetize while I was still at my job. That means instead of going out partying I was using that money for stacking. Instead of shopping I was investing. Instead of spending on liabilities I was acquiring assets.

You must figure out your "Why". "Why" do I want what I want? Is it for you or your family? Is it for your friends and associates? Is it just to look good on social media and have fun in the nightclub? You have to decide what you are making your sacrifices for. Sometimes you must sacrifice your today for your tomorrow. Learn to make small sacrifices in your daily routine and you'll see a big difference in how you view money and what's really important in your life.....

Now this is a part of sacrifice that we don't want to accept sometimes, but it's a possibility that some of the people with you now won't be with you a year or two from now. Everyone's destination in life is different and different destinations have different paths. So unfortunately, everyone won't make it to the finish line with you. At a certain point you have to make the choice that if you're going to do it you have to be in it 100%. No 1 foot in, 1 foot Out, that will only weaken your foundation. Make it clear to everyone around you what you're involved in and what you're not involved in. And learn what the phrase *Guilty by Association* means. Don't let the 99% good legit business get ruined by the 1% dirty activity! **The 99 vs 1**, Just like the little speck of dirt that can muddy up a whole glass of crystal-clear ice water and makes the entire glass useless and undrinkable.

PATIENTS

Anything worth something in life will take time to acquire. Everything is a process, and patience will help you on your journey more than anything, because it can help in business and also life. Nothing is overnight. Someone telling you you'll be rich in a month is like you telling you partner let's have sex and have a baby in a month! It doesn't work that way! Everything in the universe takes time. Time is the most beautiful thing we have, and we take it for granted every chance we get. *"We rush it to go by, but when it's gone we automatically want it back."* Enjoy it while it's here. ENJOY THE NOW! The process makes the trophy feel so much better in your hand. Things in the crock pot and stove always taste better than the food from the microwave. It's the time spent on something that makes it better. It's like taking the scenic route vs the expressway, of course you'll get there quicker on the expressway, but you'll enjoy the ride better on the scenic route, and often you'll actually be surprised by what you see or come across on your way when you take your time.

You're on no one's time but own, so don't ever feel like you're catching up or you're behind schedule. Everyone has their big break or big moment when they're supposed to, so don't ever feel like you're in a competition or a race with anyone. Bernie Mac was in his 40's when he got his big break. Morgan Freeman got famous at 52. So, just stay consistent, take your time and do it well. This is a marathon not a sprint. You're right on time.

So as was said by many great people before this generation, *make a choice or lose a chance.* Go all in with your dreams and make them your reality. You have a great idea, you have your plan, what else are you waiting on? The perfect time or opportunity will never come just knocking at your door, *"you gotta kick the damn door down and create the opportunities for yourself"*. You must have faith in your plan and in yourself. You've made the sacrifices, you have gotten your foundation built, now say a prayer and bust your Move.

The world is ready for you…

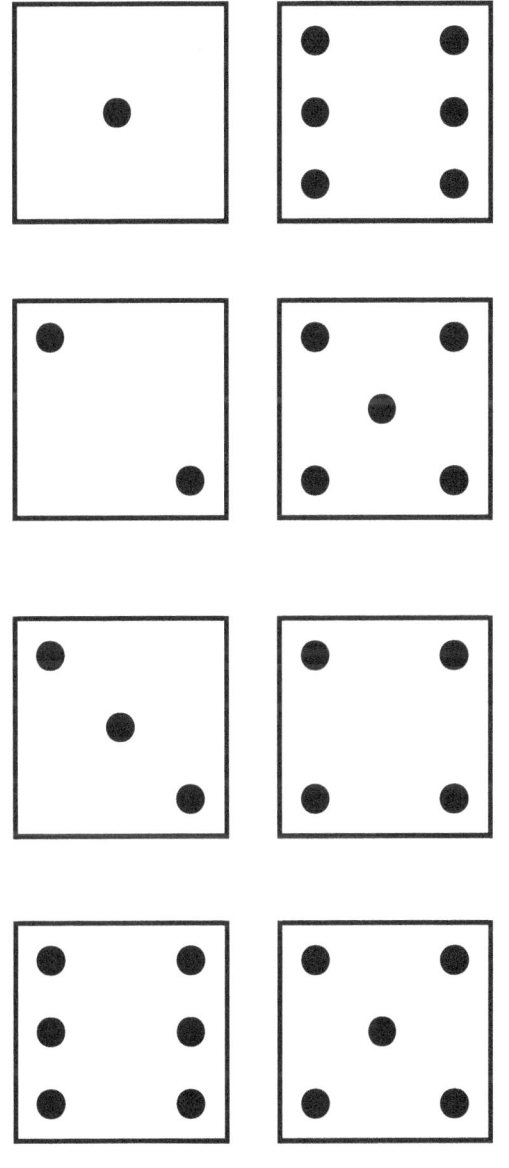

I feel blessed, I don't feel Lucky... James Prince Sr

87

CHAPTER FIVE

That's All.... JUST DO IT!!!

The 4 Check System

Now that you're on to the DOING process! You have to make sure everything is aligned and in order. Just like a brand-new sports car you have to make sure you do regularly scheduled maintenance checks on yourself. A physical check, a mental check, an emotional check and last but surely not least, a financial check. Now some people might say a financial check is not necessary to the health, but just like if you are hurting physically or emotionally, hurting financially will also change your way of thinking and eventually your decision making. Please believe if you're broke your decision making and desperation level will be 100% worse. So financial health is just as important as the rest. When you're financially healthy you make decisions on principle not money.

So look at it like this:

The 4 Check System of HEALTH

• Physical Check = Body

Exercise - Get Annual Doctor Checkups - Rest your Body

• Mental Check = Brain

Read - Meditate - Travel- Rest your Brain

• Emotional Check = Heart

Laugh - Cry - Interact- Be Present

• Financial Check = Pockets

Save - Spend - Invest - Tithe the World

So, when you are feeling bothered or out of sync do a check on yourself just like you'll check on your car. When your partner is down and not the person you recognize, do a check on them and you'll be surprised at what you discover and might be able to fix. Let's not check more on what we're driving, instead of what's drives us.

Advice - Tips & Game

At this point we know everything we need to know. We've read every book we've attended every seminar, and heard from every so-called expert on earth, so there's nothing else really for me to say. I'm just going to give you some Advice - Tips & Game that I've learned along the way that has helped me build my foundation in my life, and hopefully you'll get something out of it that will help you on your journey to Entrepreneurism.

There's no particular right or wrong way to RUN your business but there is a definite Right and wrong way to DO business.

-CONSISTENTLY

It all starts with consistency! Your dreams bring you passion and a reason for you to go hard everyday! If you had a normal job you'd **have** to wake up and go to work everyday without a choice because the fear of being fired. So why not do the same for yourself? You should always work twice as hard for your dreams and goals than working for other people's dreams at their company. You have to wake up and do it every day, all day just like them. Wal-

Mart is open every day. McDonald's is open every day. CVS doesn't Close. I know barbers who've made over a quarter million easily because their chair never closes. Consistency is key in any great business and it's a great way to build your company's reputation. People hate a lazy business owner whose business is always closed and unavailable to provide a service, don't be that business owner.

Learn the importance of a SCHEDULING it helps build consistency...

-COMPLETION

When you start something make sure to always finish and finish strong. When you have work on the plate knock it out and move on to the next job, and then the next. For example, when I get a new print order, I might tell the customer that it'll be a 1-week turnaround. But instead, I might knock it out in two or three days and contact the customer for pickup. The customer will be ecstatic and that creates 1. A great review and 2. A for sure return customer. You know a handful of people right now that always start something but never get around to completing it. Started school but never finished. Started the catering service but never got all the equipment. Got the LLC for your company but never got a logo made. Ordered 100 business cards but only handed out 25 of them. If you start something do everything in your power to complete it. People hate a half ass business owner who never delivers on what they've promised. Don't be that business owner.

Stop letting work linger SET A DEADLINE, FINISH THE JOB, AND MOVE THE HELL ON!!

-SEPARATION

Learn when to clock in and clock out. You have to figure out when to cut it off, it's a very fine line between being the prisoner and the guard. Don't let your mouth overload your body. Don't take on a workload you can't handle right now, and learn not to take your work home with you. The separation of work and home is very important. Don't bring you family to the office, don't bring your briefcase to the beach. Enjoy the time with your family while you have it, time is the most important thing on earth we have. The money can always be replaced and remade, but time is gone once it's gone. When a person is close to death they never say, "Man I wish I had more money". The wish is always for more time. So close that laptop and detach from the work and pay attention to the now. I know business owners that work-work-work so much that they can't even produce the workload they've took in and they can't even enjoy the money their making. So don't overwork yourself. Busy and productive are two different things. Activity is not achievement! Don't confuse the two. Don't mix your business time with your personal time. Don't be that business owner.

DONT STRECH YOURSELF THIN
Don't let other people's mistakes become your emergency

Your problem can't be my problem if my solution isn't your

Solution... - James Mitchell
(1983 - 2022)

Money Management

Money management is KEY in any entrepreneurial or management situation for the simple fact "when you need it, YOU NEED IT!! Proper money management practices might save your life during a rainy day, if a quick investment opportunity pops up, or in an emergency family situation. Spend on assets not liabilities, my motto is "*not a dollar spent but a dollar invested*". Needs must be priority over wants, and *Bills* and *Taxes* must be paid First!, that's just the cost of doing business unfortunately. It's easy to overspend when you first start doing good but really that's when you have to be the most disciplined in your spending. When your output exceeds your income, your upkeep can become your downfall.

Minimizing bills and expenses is key in the process of financial health. Learn and practice different ways of saving and investing money. Try gathering different assets that will make your money grow instead of buying things that will just take your money with no return on your dollar. Relationships with your local bank can be a great way to get information about different avenues of managing your money. Such as checking and saving accounts, business credit, business funding, etc.

Take your Time and Save your Money! Practice discipline. Instead of celebrating your first sale, save that money and celebrate the 1-year Anniversary of your business. Don't clap for winning the battle, celebrate winning the War!!

Now Go Do It...

We've done all the Studying, all the planning and preparing, all the saving and made our choice...

Now start DOING it!

Rule #1
Get The Money 1st
Rule #2
Don't forget to get the money

-Adolph Thornton Jr
(1985 - 2021)

OUTRO

Now that you've shifted your **MINDSET (Chapter 1)**, created, and structured your **PLAN (Chapter 2)**, Built you a Strong **FOUNDATION (Chapter 3)**, and made your **CHOICE (Chapter 4)**. The only thing to do now is to start **DOING (Chapter 5)**. If you think it, you can do it. Simple and plain! Literally everything around us started as a thought. An idea, a dream, no matter how crazy it sounded, no matter the amount of time or resources it took to get the idea done, somehow, it got done.

Richard Montanez - Flaming Hot Cheetos

Wright brothers – The Airplane

Johannes Gutenberg – The Printing Press

Madam C.J. Walker – The First Hair Products

Garrett Morgan – The Traffic Light

Steve Jobs – Founded Apple

From the fire to the microwave. From the horse and carriage wooden wagons to the electric cars we drive today. *Somebody had to create that shit Mane...* **WHY NOT ONE OF US!** All those examples started with a dream somebody had, and they woke up and made that shit happen. Looking back at shows like The Jetsons and Star Trek with all the flatscreen TVs, flying vehicles and the kitchen electronics that we all thought were insane 20 to 30 years ago. Fast forward all these years later they have televisions inside of refrigerators. All these things became reality because of someone's thoughts, someone's vision, someone's dream. No idea is too big or small, in fact, the bigger the better!

Most authors in the books I read, the authors I'm recommended or the so called "GURUS", all seem to me to like their talking from a stage and have never been a part of the audience. Like I said, I'm writing this book from the point of view of someone who has been at the lowest of the low and use my own two feet to build multiple businesses. I can tell you 100% without a shadow of a doubt if I can do it, ANYONE can do it. I had every excuse, Black Male "Check", single mom "Check", crime infested city "Check", kicked out of multiple schools "Check", medical diagnosed learning disorder "Check", F student "Check", arrest record "Check", flat dirt broke "Check". I had every excuse possible at my fingertips and could've used any one of them to give up, but I didn't and I'm grateful every day that I changed my **MINDSET** and my life. My motto is "*If you think it, you can Do it*" Simple!

I use to ride the MATA bus to the blood bank to donate blood for $45. Spend $20 for my weed habit, $20 on court fines, and with that $5 left in my pocket I STILL had the Mindset to know one day I would be successful. I didn't know exactly **how** or **when** but knew 100% that I **was** going to make it. Most situations we find ourselves in are self-inflicted, and with realistic self-awareness we can avoid a lot of these situations. Some situations that we're born into are out of our control like poverty, disability, no parental guidance, but YOU yourself have the ability to create any path you choose to become successful. Just like the people who are born in great situations with rich parents, child acting stars, or that straight "A" student we all know who ended up unsuccessful and sometimes tragic. The tools were available for them to be successful, but the MINDSET wasn't there. On the other hand, if the MINDSET is there then you can acquire the tools needed along the way to make your dreams become reality. Like many rags to riches stories, we've heard in the past.

Right now, at this moment I'm literally writing this at the airport in Minnesota where I just spent the last 2 weeks in isolation, peace and adventure. I wrote part of chapter 5 at Lake Wacona, this being my first time in Minnesota, I discovered their state was known as "The Land of 10,000

Lakes" and before I left, I made it my goal to see at least 100 and I came damn close. I'm headed back home to Memphis not because I have to, but because I want to. I can take a flight from here and go anywhere I want and spend as long as I want. Not because I'm the riches or anything like that, but I made my choice a long time ago that I would work for my freedom, my time, and my life on my terms.

Remember this before I leave….

Always know what exactly you want out of every situation.

Never feel Rushed or Pressured by anyone or anything your Time is your Time! Use it wisely….

Never stop learning new and old ways of the world.

Learn from people, life, and the world

Your brain works like any other muscle, so exercise it or that mother fucker will become weak as hell…. And people prey on the weak.

Never depend on anyone for anything, enjoy your friends and family. Love them but don't Need them….

*Never stop **Working**, Never stop **Hustling**, Never stop **Thinking**, Never stop **Smashing**…*

THE END

I just wrote a book on these folks' ass!

ENTREPRENEURISM

P	N	D	P	Y	B	I	C	P	Y	Y	T	E	R	S
R	E	N	Y	L	F	H	E	E	N	M	E	R	U	I
O	T	A	L	N	A	E	N	A	I	Y	U	E	E	H
P	W	R	T	N	D	O	P	N	O	H	M	T	N	P
E	O	B	C	G	M	M	D	L	Q	L	N	I	E	M
R	R	E	G	J	O	S	P	E	U	Y	O	R	R	E
Q	K	O	W	C	E	M	B	D	I	X	I	E	P	M
K	D	F	W	T	E	X	G	U	Z	E	T	M	E	C
T	I	O	D	T	S	U	J	Q	S	V	A	E	R	H
G	N	I	T	E	K	R	A	M	A	I	D	N	T	O
A	I	N	T	I	T	M	A	N	E	W	N	T	N	I
J	E	D	U	C	A	T	I	O	N	C	U	E	E	C
D	O	I	N	G	A	S	N	A	L	P	O	N	S	E
I	N	V	E	S	T	I	N	G	G	W	F	Q	V	S
D	O	O	G	S	I	D	O	G	V	X	I	A	Y	G

1. ENTREPRENEUR
2. MINDSET
3. PLAN
4. FOUNDATION
5. CHOICE
6. DOING
7. BUSINESS
8. EDUCATION
9. MARKETING
10. INVESTING
11. EMPLOYEE
12. BRAND
13. COMPANY
14. NETWORK
15. CHANCE
16. MONEY
17. RETIREMENT
18. GodIsGood
19. JustDoIt
20. AintItMane
21. HIDDEN WORD (6 LETTERS)
22. HIDDEN WORD (7 LETTERS)
23. HIDDEN WORD (8 LETTERS)

ENTREPR

@Entrepreneur.izm
Entrepreneurizm.com
@EnterprizePrinting
EnterprizePrinting.com
@EnterprizeLenzs
@DoggDeepENT
DoggDeep.com
@TrojoCal

ENEURiizzmM